SPOTTING DIFFERENCES

Turtle
or
Tortoise?

by Kirsten Chang

BLASTOFF! READERS

BELLWETHER MEDIA • MINNEAPOLIS, MN

Note to Librarians, Teachers, and Parents:

Blastoff! Readers are carefully developed by literacy experts and combine standards-based content with developmentally appropriate text.

Level 1 provides the most support through repetition of high-frequency words, light text, predictable sentence patterns, and strong visual support.

Level 2 offers early readers a bit more challenge through varied simple sentences, increased text load, and less repetition of high-frequency words.

Level 3 advances early-fluent readers toward fluency through increased text and concept load, less reliance on visuals, longer sentences, and more literary language.

Level 4 builds reading stamina by providing more text per page, increased use of punctuation, greater variation in sentence patterns, and increasingly challenging vocabulary.

Level 5 encourages children to move from "learning to read" to "reading to learn" by providing even more text, varied writing styles, and less familiar topics.

Whichever book is right for your reader, Blastoff! Readers are the perfect books to build confidence and encourage a love of reading that will last a lifetime!

This edition first published in 2020 by Bellwether Media, Inc.

No part of this publication may be reproduced in whole or in part without written permission of the publisher. For information regarding permission, write to Bellwether Media, Inc., Attention: Permissions Department, 6012 Blue Circle Drive, Minnetonka, MN 55343.

Library of Congress Cataloging-in-Publication Data

Names: Chang, Kirsten, 1991- author.
Title: Turtle or Tortoise? / by Kirsten Chang.
Description: Minneapolis, MN : Bellwether Media, Inc., [2020] | Series: Blastoff! Readers: Spotting Differences |
    Audience: Age 5-8. | Audience: K to Grade 3. | Includes bibliographical references and index.
Identifiers: LCCN 2018056030 (print) | LCCN 2018056494 (ebook) | ISBN 9781618915771 (ebook) |
    ISBN 9781644870365 (hardcover : alk. paper)
Subjects: LCSH: Turtles--Juvenile literature. | Testudinidae--Juvenile literature.
Classification: LCC QL666.C5 (ebook) | LCC QL666.C5 C556 2020 (print) | DDC 597.92--dc23
LC record available at https://lccn.loc.gov/2018056030

Editor: Al Albertson   Designer: Jeffrey Kollock

Printed in the United States of America, North Mankato, MN.

Table of Contents

Turtles and Tortoises

Turtles and tortoises are **reptiles**. They both have **shells** on their backs.

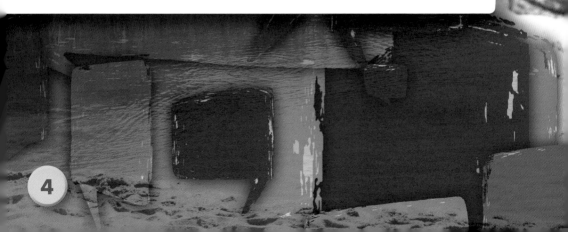

tortoise

shell

Turtles and tortoises
are in the same family.
How are they different?

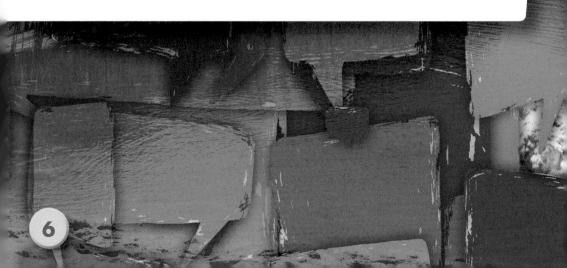

turtles

Different Looks

Tortoises have round shells. Most turtles have flat shells.

Turtles have front legs that act like **flippers**. Many turtles have **webbed** feet.

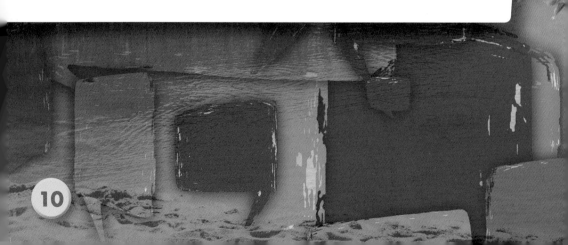

**webbed
foot**

Tortoises have legs
like elephants.
Their round legs
end in flat feet.

Different Lives

Turtles spend most of their lives in water. Flippers help them swim.

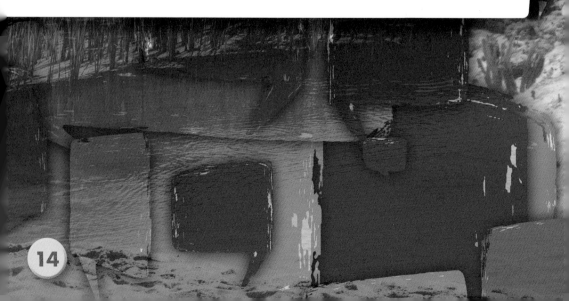

Tortoises live on land.
They cannot swim.

Tortoises only eat plants.
Turtles eat plants and
animals. Can you tell
the difference?

flat shell

webbed feet

front feet
like flippers

Turtle Differences

spend most of
their lives in water

eat plants
and animals

round
shell

flat feet

round legs

Tortoise Differences

spend their
lives on land

eat plants

Glossary

flippers

wide, flat limbs used for swimming

shells

the hard coverings of some animals

reptiles

cold-blooded animals that lay eggs

webbed

having thin skin that connects the toes

To Learn More

AT THE LIBRARY

Black, Vanessa. *Tortoises*. Minneapolis, Minn.: Bullfrog Books, 2017.

Herrington, Lisa M. *Turtles and Tortoises*. New York, N.Y.: Children's Press, 2016.

Ryndak, Rob. *Turtle or Tortoise?* New York, N.Y.: Gareth Stevens Publishing, 2016.

ON THE WEB

FACTSURFER

Factsurfer.com gives you a safe, fun way to find more information.

1. Go to www.factsurfer.com.

2. Enter "turtle or tortoise" into the search box and click 🔍.

3. Select your book cover to see a list of related web sites.

Index

The images in this book are reproduced through the courtesy of: Korkin Vadim, front cover (turtle); FOTOGRIN, front cover (tortoise), pp. 12-13; Jenny Sturm, pp. 4-5; uxman tahir, pp. 6-7, 8-9; Paul Reeves Photography, p. 9 (bubble); Sally Wallis, pp. 10-11; Patryk Kosmider, pp. 14-15; nwdph, pp. 16-17; Ivan Kuzmin/ Alamy, pp. 18-19; Baishev, p. 20 (turtle); Bruce MacQueen, p. 20 (eat plants/animals); Eric Isselee, p. 21 (tortoise); NagyDodo, p. 21 (spend time on land); seasoning_17, pp. 21 (eat plants), 22 (reptiles); Davdeka, p. 22 (flippers); Lynette Knott Rudman, p. 22 (shells); fztommy, p. 22 (webbed).